# ISA POCKET GUIDES

# COMING TO GRIPS WITH HOMO-SEXUALITY

# COMING TO GRIPS WITH HOMO-SEXUALITY

## ERWIN W. LUTZER

**MOODY PRESS**
CHICAGO

© 1991 by
THE MOODY BIBLE INSTITUTE
OF CHICAGO

All rights reserved. No part of this book may be reproduced in any form without permission in writing from the publisher, except in the case of brief quotations embodied in critical articles or reviews.

All Scripture quotations, unless noted otherwise, are from the *New American Standard Bible*, © 1960, 1962, 1963, 1968, 1972, 1972, 1973, 1975, and 1977 by The Lockman Foundation, and are used by permission.

Some of the material in this booklet appeared initially in *Living with Your Passion* (Wheaton, Ill.: Victor, 1983), by Erwin W. Lutzer, and is used by permission of the publisher.

ISBN: 0-8024-3548-3

1 2 3 4 5 6 7 Printing/VP/Year 95 94 93 92 91

*Printed in the United States of America*

# Coming to Grips with
# Homosexuality

There was a time when the church thought it did not have to address the subject of homosexuality. The mistaken belief was that only few people exhibited sexual desire toward the same sex. Today with homosexuality receiving so much attention, no one can ignore the struggles of many (yes, Christians too) who find themselves driven with desires they do not want to have but cannot seem to change. We must realize that homosexuals are everywhere, including in our churches.

Unfortunately, issues of sexuality have often been ignored by Christians, evidently under the pretext that if we do not mention a problem, it does not exist. But sexuality is so much a part of us that it cannot be ignored without devastating consequences.

The term *homosexual* applies to either men or women who are erotically attracted toward members of their own sex, though often the word *lesbian* is used to designate a female homosexual. Most homosexuals call themselves "gays" in order to convey the impression that the homosexual lifestyle is filled with carefree pleasures (gay, as in happy).

Unfortunately, society has coined other descriptive terms, such as *fag, weird,* or *queer;* these are frequently used in derision of homosexuals. Such language only contributes to deepening the chasm of misunderstanding between homosexuals and heterosexuals (those who are attracted to the opposite sex).

Who can imagine the pain that is felt by those who are the object of such uncaring, unchristian remarks? If homosexuals cannot turn to Christ and His people for love and understanding, where should they go? A judgmental, uncaring attitude has driven countless people deeper into homosexual patterns and behavior. Few groups in society have faced as much condemnation from the church as homosexuals. We all know that Christ came into the world to save sinners, but often the impression is given that homosexuals are excluded from His love and grace. Such a gospel is unworthy of the name.

Why this prejudice against homosexuals? One reason is a lack of perspective. Many people thoughtlessly associate all homosexuals with the radical gay rights activists, who are determined to force homosexual values on society by intimidation and political activism. But those groups do not represent all homosexuals, indeed perhaps they speak for only a fraction of the homosexual population. Most suffer silently, searching for sexual wholeness. More of that later.

Second, heterosexuals who consider homosexuality abhorrent underestimate the depths of confusion and pain connected with homosexuality. Superficial comments such as "Why doesn't he get married?" reveal deep insensitivity toward the needs, thoughts, and feelings of the homosexual. If we would take the time to understand the pain and sense of rejection that they endure, we would be sympathetic. They have the same need for love and understanding as all people do, perhaps more so. Many of them attempt to meet these legitimate needs through homosexual relationships.

Put yourself in the shoes of a homosexual: You are a male eighteen years old. You have powerful erotic attractions to men. You do not think that you have chosen this lifestyle. At puberty your desires began to be directed toward the same sex. Your friends are attracted to girls, but you are not interested. The pressure of society and your own feelings remind you that you are abnormal; your peers call you "weird." You try to change but you cannot. You implore God for help, but your passions continue unabated.

What would you do?

Tell your parents? They might not understand. In fact, one organization established to help parents of homosexual children is called the Spatula Club because parents need to be scraped off the ceiling when they hear news of their child's homosexuality!

Tell your pastor? Not if he berates homosexuals from the pulpit. You have no idea what he might say to you. And even if he doesn't say it, you know how he feels.

A common response of homosexuals is to seek out others with whom they can identify. If they are Christians they may seek out other homosexuals within the church. Those who are not Christians may find friends among those who are openly homosexual. Once the homosexual lifestyle is begun, the pattern of behavior generally continues.

Understandably, many homosexuals are bitter because they do not think that the church understands them. Many of them have written

Christianity off, thinking that the church can provide only condemnation. Most are angry with God too, believing that He is to blame for their sexual identity. They think this is the card they have been dealt.

No one should speak about homosexuality without a caring heart. I doubt whether anyone ever changed his sexual identity simply because he heard a sermon condemning homosexuality. The teaching of Scripture must be accompanied by understanding, patience, and love. David Augsburger has wisely said, "It is so much easier to tell a person what to do with his problem than to stand with him in his pain."

Homosexuals are well aware of the stereotypes and hostility that others may feel toward them. And even if those feelings are not present within a congregation, many homosexuals will think that they exist. Here, as in other relationships, perception is often reality.

As already indicated, it is essential to distinguish between avowed homosexuals and those who struggle with homosexuality, knowing that the lifestyle is sinful, but are unable to change. Although this booklet is written primarily to offer hope to those who wish to be freed from homosexuality, this important distinction must be discussed in more detail.

## THE QUEST FOR HOMOSEXUAL RIGHTS

Some Christian leaders have been criticized for being publicly opposed to "gay rights." Such opposition, we are told, is contrary to the love of Christ and therefore creates a stumbling block in the homosexual community.

However, we must understand the difference between the two groups, the militant homosexuals who are bent on transforming society and the individual who has no intention of using legislation to impose his lifestyle on others.

To summarize: the "Gay Rights Movement" refers to those within the homosexual community who have organized to impose homosexual values on all of society. They are proud to be homosexuals, insisting that they have the right to change society through political action and a sympathetic media.

This movement is so powerful that it has the ability to make demands of psychiatrists, politicians, and health experts and get exactly what it wants.

Consider the gains the movement has made in recent years. (1) In 1974 the Gay Rights Movement persuaded the American Psychiatric Association to drop homosexuality as a sexual deviation. Militant activists disrupted psychiatric meetings, made demands of psychiatrists, and pressured the members to make the change. One prominent psychiatrist said that it was the first time in psychiatric history that a scientific society ignored scientific evidence and yielded to the demands of a militant group (*Psychiatric Annals*, April 1976).

Then (2) homosexuals have lobbied to pass ordinances that give special privileges to homosexuals in the schools, apartment complexes, and the workplace. Under the banner of equality, homosexuality must be taught in the schools as a legitimate alternate lifestyle; landlords and employers no longer have the right to decide whether a person's sexual preference might have relevance in renting an apartment or in the workplace. Even organizations such as Big Brothers have been forced to accept homosexuals as prospective "brothers" to fatherless youth. When this happens a boy's mother no longer has the right to choose what kind of "brother" her child would have if she wished to join the organization.

Homosexuals are seeking the right to legitimize their marriages and to adopt children. The plan is that eventually churches will be forced to hire homosexuals to meet the demands of equal employment. One domino after another is falling as the courts give expansive rights to the homosexual cause.

Also (3) the homosexual movement has opposed specialists in the medical field who years ago insisted that those who have AIDS be quarantined to protect society. By opposing such health precautions and tirelessly campaigning for freedom to practice various forms of sexual behavior, these radicals have in effect defended the right to infect others with a deadly disease.

This crusade was conducted under the banner of civil rights, implying that their struggle was essentially the same as the right of blacks to be regarded as equal members of society. Incredibly, many people, though not personally accepting this misrepresentation, have been silenced through fear of being branded "homophobic." (For the details read *Exposing the AIDS Scandal*, by Paul Cameron [Lafayette, La.: Huntington, 1988].)

Then (4) they have successfully used intimidation to control the media and the public health officials of the United States. At a recent AIDS conference, the presence of homosexuals was noisy and persistent. They cheered and applauded speakers who agreed with them and booed and hissed those who said things that were contrary to their cause. Health considerations were to be subservient to the the homosexual agenda.

When a news commentator made an innocuous comment about homosexuality, he was forced to resign and reinstated only when he apologized to the gay community. So powerful is their intimidation of the media that an objective report on homosexuality is virtually impossible.

As already emphasized, such outspoken homosexuals make it difficult for those who struggle with homosexuality to "come out of the closet" for fear that they will be identified with the radicals.

However, *the legitimate opposition we might have toward these militant spokespersons cannot be transferred to the person who is frightened into suffering in silence.* Let it never be said that we have turned our backs on anyone, homosexual or heterosexual, who seeks the love and compassion of Christ.

That does not mean that we should reinterpret the Bible to suit the prevailing cultural mind-set. It does mean that we try to understand those suffering with a homosexual orientation and listen to what they have to say, feel their rejection, and identify with their anger and disappointments.

This book is dedicated to those who struggle with homosexuality as

Christians, those who know that homosexual behavior is contrary to the Bible but think they are powerless to change. I also write for those who have discarded Christianity in the mistaken belief that Christ has no relevance to their lifestyle.

### LEVELS OF HOMOSEXUAL STRUGGLE

When we speak of homosexuality we must remember that the term encompasses a broad range of feelings and behaviors. It is best to view homosexuality on a continuum, allowing for many different levels of desire or involvement.

First, there is the person who feels confusion about his sexual identity. He might have attraction to the same sex, and he fears that he might be a homosexual. This experience may be just a phase, a natural curiosity and arousal that need not determine his future sexual identity.

As we shall see later, at puberty teenagers can be ambivalent in their sexual feelings. The decisions that are made in adolescence will play a large role in their future sexual focus. These young people must realize that they are not locked into homosexual fantasies and experiences. Knowing that they are not programmed to be homosexuals will free them from the hopelessness that often accompanies those feelings.

Second, there is the person who has bisexual feelings, that is, who feels sexual attraction to both sexes. Such an individual must realize that his sexual bent will be determined by choice and not some prior, inborn disposition. He must know that his sexual identity will develop according to the fantasies and behavior he adopts. Whatever sexual drive is pursued will determine its ultimate expression.

Making the transition from a homosexual focus to a heterosexual one is much easier when fantasies have not given way to sexual acts. Homosexual encounters make an almost indelible impression upon the soul that makes such behavior more difficult to overcome. The reasons for this will be explained later.

Third, there is the person who has had homosexual encounters and has come to enjoy those relationships, however unnatural they may have appeared to be at first. After the line has been crossed, those experiences begin to occupy his attention, and he accepts homosexual behavior as a lifestyle. Initially he wished he could change, but now he thinks that there is no way out of his immoral patterns. But he continues to hope that perhaps someday he will be able to walk away from it all. The more open he is to change the better.

Finally, there is the person who wholeheartedly accepts homosexuality and does not desire change. He feels no guilt and is content with homosexual relationships. He has convinced himself that homosexuality is morally equivalent to heterosexuality, or perhaps even superior. He either does not care what the Bible teaches or he will reinterpret it to suit his preference.

Many homosexuals would not change their sexual identity even if they could. They are content with their partners and have a feeling of acceptance and security within those relationships. The thought of leaving homosexuality behind is no longer an option.

### THE NATURE OF SEXUALITY

We cannot understand homosexuality without coming to grips with the more general topic of sexuality. You and I are sexual beings, created with strong desires that need direction and control. Our sexual identity is at the very core of who we are as people.

Sex is not merely a pleasurable biological experience, but the act actually binds two people together, body, soul, and spirit. Sex joins two personalities into one bond that is not easily broken.

Even sex without any commitment, sex with a prostitute, begets a unity that properly belongs to marriage. Paul wrote, "Or do you not know that the one who joins himself to a harlot is one body with her? For He says, 'The two shall become one flesh'" (1 Corinthians 6:16). Notice that Paul uses the language of Genesis 2:24 (the reference is to the marriage of Adam and Eve), to describe what happens when a man has a sexual relationship with a harlot.

This does not mean that sexual intercourse binds two people together in marriage, for marriage is protected by a covenant. But the bonding that takes place is the same as that which occurs between a man and his wife.

Any sexual relationship, whether homosexual or heterosexual, binds two people together in an intimate union that has far-reaching consequences. There is evidence that God created both male and female simply because both sexes are needed to complete the image of God that we all have stamped upon us. In marriage the image of God is therefore clearly to be seen.

Marriage between a man and a woman is designed to protect this union; the intention of God is that no other person should come between the two who have been joined together in holy matrimony. The particular nature of a man and woman is thus preserved, and the most intimate relationship on earth finds its fulfillment.

A homosexual relationship, like an adulterous relationship, creates an alien bond that of necessity has lasting and detrimental consequences. The unity of two people outside of God's prescribed will eventually increases emptiness and confusion.

What are the results of this alien bonding that occurs in relationships outside of a man/woman marriage?

The first consequence is *guilt*. Modern society delights in denying that there is guilt as a result of these relationships; or else the argument is that guilt is a feeling that must simply be unlearned.

Not so. Try as they might, those who have illicit sexual relationships will experience at least some guilt, which is often sublimated and therefore emerges in other negative emotions, such as anger, depression, or a sense of unfulfillment. Alien bonds are often accompanied by alcohol or drug abuse to deaden the pain of this guilt.

A second consequence is *promiscuity*, the tendency to seek other relationships that will only increase the frustration and guilt. People have no strong commitment to maintain faithfulness to an alien bond. Because of the inherent betrayal these alien bonds perpetuate, the person is driven to seek other relationships, looking for the satisfaction that cannot be found. Thus a cycle of immorality begins.

This explains why the first sexual relationship often will determine the direction of a person's sexual future. Young people who are promiscuous before marriage will not only have the temptation to continue that lifestyle after marriage, but they must cope with the frustration of having the image of a number of other people stamped upon their souls. This produces psychological confusion and unfulfillment.

Those who are introduced to homosexuality by an older companion will have that experience stamped so indelibly upon their souls that they will eventually have the temptation to pursue more of the same. Because the bond created was illicit, they will not find permanent fulfillment in the relationship and so will seek a whole series of sexual companions, seeking what is now impossible to find.

Each successive sexual experience superimposes itself upon the previous one, each relationship vying for allegiance. Yet with so many relationships, the human personality is fragmented, unable to cope with the sense of frustration produced by a multitude of encounters. The victim is therefore driven into more sexual relationships, seeking the fulfillment that now must of necessity elude him/her. Often the result is that he gives himself over to lust, pursuing relationships with abandon.

This explains why homosexuals (or heterosexual adulterers, for that matter), think they are locked into their particular kind of sexual behavior. Their desires are heightened by their pursuit of what they of necessity cannot find; they are convinced that they are enjoying life simply because they try to compensate for their emptiness by pursuing the perfect person they long to connect with.

With the spread of AIDS it was discovered that the average male homosexual admitted to having about 550 sexual partners, many having had thousands of relationships. Some homosexuals said that they had as many as 10 or 15 homosexual experiences in a single evening in a bath or gay bar. An average of 2 or 3 new partners a week is not excessive.

This explains why the path leading out of homosexuality is fraught with many battles and temptations. The person who has given himself to homosexuality finds it difficult to master the desires he has so often obeyed.

### THE CAUSES OF HOMOSEXUALITY

We must resist the tendency to think that every homosexual fits into a neat stereotype, but there is strong evidence that general patterns emerge when we try to identify the cause of homosexuality.

First, there is the family. According to Dr. George Rekers, "The fathers of homosexual sons are most often described as being aloof, hostile, and rejecting. More than four-fifths of adult male homosexuals report that their fathers were physically or psychologically absent from their homes while they were growing up."[1] These young men lacked strong, healthy male role models; consequently their own sexual identity became confused. They simply could not relate meaningfully to the opposite sex. Often a passive or absentee father accompanies an overprotective, dominant mother in the home. The boy thus identifies with his mother and assumes her sexual role. One former homosexual told me, "My mother dressed me in girls' clothes. At school the kids said, 'He

1. *Growing Up Straight* (Chicago: Moody, 1982), p. 68. Hereafter cited in the text.

must be queer.' I thought they must be right and I began to think about my identity. Soon I pursued relationships with other males."

If a mother hates men and communicates this to her son, she may make the boy vulnerable to homosexual temptations. Particularly in the absence of a man in the home, the boy might begin to shrink from the male role that he should identify with. No one can calculate the amount of damage that hostility between parents contributes to the confusion of sex roles.

Child abuse also contributes to the reversal of sex roles. If a girl was molested by her father, she may develop an aversion toward men that may drive her into lesbianism. To quote Rekers again, "Certain kinds of families can leave a child with unresolved emotional conflict or with feelings that tempt him to pursue a shortcut to intimacy by having sexual relations with a person of the same sex" (p. 67).

A second cause is sexual exploitation. Almost all children are at some time sexually stimulated by thinking about, or seeing, someone of the same sex. For most, it is a fleeting experience. But if those feelings are exploited, they may persist and develop into a homosexual orientation. Psychologists tell us that at the age of puberty a child is particularly impressionable, and if he or she begins to focus on the same sex, homosexual desires are intensified. Understandably, homosexual pornography contributes to inflaming those desires and helps to solidify the direction of the victim's sexual preference.

It is difficult to obtain accurate statistics on how many people are now homosexuals because they were recruited. Roger Montgomery, who died of AIDS on November 6, 1989, was a homosexual prostitute who estimates that he had sexual encounters with between 1,000 and 1,500 different men. He often asked his partners how they got into the homosexual lifestyle. By far the majority said that they had been recruited by a neighbor, a friend, or a relative. Usually, this was accompanied by the use of pornography. In his case, this happened when he was molested by a neighbor at the age of six.

Sexual exploitation of children and the widespread number of dysfunctional families make up the soil in which homosexuality most easily grows. Teenagers who do not have the benefit of a family that gives them a strong sense of personal identity often withdraw from pursuing normal relationships and gravitate to the same sex, where they do not feel threatened. Because they are so impressionable, they can focus on the same sex, and this continues to lead them into homosexuality.

From within all of us comes a deep desire to be loved and understood. Those who are denied that sense of security and intimacy will be tempted to find it among those who appear to accept them. Whether homosexual or heterosexual, the child who grows up feeling unloved will tend to seek sexual intimacy with a partner, or partners, without the benefit of marriage.

Men and women struggling with a homosexual orientation are particularly driven by the need to be loved and accepted. But because they are convinced that they cannot relate to the opposite sex, they pursue same-sex relationships. That is why there can be no true freedom from homosexuality without the love and support of others. The very thing homosexuals so desperately need is what Christians have been most reluctant to give them, namely, love and acceptance (without condoning the lifestyle).

### THE BIBLE AND HOMOSEXUALITY

The Bible clearly teaches that homosexuality is sin, but it makes equally clear that deliverance is possible. Both of these truths must be proclaimed to our society.

In the Old Testament a number of offenses were punishable by death. Among them were adultery and homosexuality. Specifically, God says, "If there is a man who lies with a male as those who lie with a woman, both of them have committed a detestable act; they shall surely be put to death. Their bloodguiltiness is on them (Leviticus 20:13).

In Romans 1:26-27 we read that homosexuality is against nature. "For this reason God gave them over to degrading passions; for their women exchanged the natural function for that which is unnatural, and in the same way also the men abandoned the natural function of the woman and burned in their desire toward one another, men with men committing indecent acts and receiving in their own bodies the due penalty of their error." That statement means that the homosexual is fighting against the nature of his own body. This is confirmed by Paul's use of the words *exchanged* and *abandoned*. The homosexual has abandoned what his body normally craves. Associated with this transformation are guilt and fear, which often drive the person to pursue further homosexual relationships. When Paul says, "God gave them over," he means that God delivers a person over to sin by intensifying the guilt and desire in a person's life. At this point he (or she) either will be brought to complete repentance or will be driven even more intensely by passions. Paul speaks of homosexuals burning toward one another, an apt description of homosexual passion.

Some evangelicals say that homosexuality must be accepted as an alternate sexual preference. They make a distinction between homosexual acts, which result from a conscious choice on the part of the individual, and homosexual orientation. Those who take this view believe some are born with homosexual tendencies and therefore cannot be held accountable for their "preference."

Of course there is a difference between homosexual behavior and homosexual lust, just as there is a difference between heterosexual lust and behavior, but that does not mean that homosexual desires are normal. Rekers writes: "All homosexual lust is abnormal and fights against normal sexual adjustment. Each instance of homosexual lust conditions the nervous system to an even stronger responsiveness to homosexual stimulation" (p. 24).

The Bible is clear that both homosexual acts and homosexual lusts are sinful and a perversion of God's will for men and women. It may be natural for a person to be a kleptomaniac, but that does not mean that those desires should be accepted as moral. Even homosexuals themselves admit that their desires are contrary to nature.

Dr. Armond Nicholai, chief psychiatrist of the Medical School at Harvard University and editor of the *Harvard Guide to Psychiatry*, said: "I have treated hundreds of homosexuals. None of them, deep down, thought he was normal. Simulating eating is not eating. Simulating being female is not being female. Simulating sex is not sex."[2]

Some people think that they were born a homosexual because are not aware of any conscious step or experience that caused them to become a homosexual. But in such instances decisions were made and behavior pursued that led the individual to abandon his natural desires in favor of homosexual preferences.

But, as we shall see, that does not mean that a person has to continue to follow those desires. Ruth Barnhouse, a Christian psychotherapist,

2. Quoted in "Are Gay Rights Rights? A Report on Homosexuality and the Law," by Roger Magnuson (Minneapolis, Minn.: The Berean League), p. 21.

wrote: "The process of psychotherapy entails a very large element of helping the sufferer to understand that he is not a victim of something beyond himself, but that choices made in the past, however unconsciously, can be reviewed and new decisions taken."

Some people do grow up with homosexual desires because of environmental factors, usually coupled with specific experiences that made them vulnerable to the redirection of their sexual passions. But there is no evidence that anyone is born a homosexual.

Given the fact that the family is the key to developing healthy relationships, we must lament the breakdown of this institution in American life. We've heard it said that God will someday judge America because we have sinned against great light. We expect huge earthquakes or famine. But actually, America is already being judged with a punishment much more severe than those natural phenomena. The final judgment on Israel was the scattering of families (Deuteronomy 28:64).

The emotional consequences of divorce on children are much more severe than a natural disaster could ever be. Little wonder God's last Old Testament word to mankind regarding the coming of John the Baptist included these words: "And he will restore the hearts of the fathers to their children, and the hearts of the children to their fathers, lest I come and smite the earth with a curse" (Malachi 4:6).

With the breakup of our homes and the harsh and unloving attitudes of some parents toward each other and their children, it is not surprising that we have many who feel the pangs of rejection and hurt. Nor is it surprising that some of these individuals are driven by their inner desires to sinful relationships as a shortcut to intimacy. It is no wonder that homosexuality is on the increase.

Those who live with a homosexual orientation are wounded people. They have been so deeply scarred that they are sensitive to the attitudes and feelings of others. They often disassociate themselves from Christians for fear of being rejected. Unfortunately, that also means that they may be quick to take up an offense and harbor bitterness.

For those who admit their need, we must offer support and encouragement. Who among us has never been bound by a sin that was brought on by the failures of those who have influenced us the most? Homosexuality is only one of many consequences of sin in our fallen world.

Is there a way out?

Evangelicals are divided on whether or not Christ actually changes homosexuals into heterosexuals. Because many revert to homosexuality after extensive counseling, some believe we should have a less ambitious goal. The most we can expect, they say, is to teach them to resist temptation. Once an alcoholic, always an alcoholic; once a homosexual, always a homosexual in basic orientation, they say. The goal should be to strengthen them so that they will not be involved in homosexual activity even though they still have homosexual desires.

To pursue this argument further: just as single heterosexuals must learn to curb their passions and abstain from sexual relationships, so a homosexual must learn to live in celibacy. Since all of us are required to say no to lust, it really does not matter whether our lust is homosexual or heterosexual. In either case the same biblical teaching applies: "Do not let sin reign in your mortal body that you should obey its lusts" (Romans 6:12).

Freedom from homosexual acts is important as a first step. Some will be content to be celibate in their relationships, without thinking that they need to actually see a change in the direction of their desires.

But I believe God is able to take a person beyond that to an actual redirection of his or her desires. When Paul discussed various kinds of sinners who had put their past behind them, he included homosexuals:

> Or do you not know that the unrighteous shall not inherit the kingdom of God? Do not be deceived; neither fornicators, nor idolaters, nor adulterers, nor effeminate, nor homosexuals, nor thieves, nor the covetous, nor drunkards, nor revilers, nor swindlers, shall inherit the kingdom of God. And such were some of you; but you were washed, but you were sanctified, but you were justified in name of the Lord Jesus Christ, and in the Spirit of our God." (1 Corinthians 6:9-11)

Paul affirmed that God had delivered them from their preconversion lifestyles. In the Corinthian church there were those who had put their homosexuality behind them.

Of course it is not an easy journey. The homosexual who is a believer must rejoice in God's love toward him and realize that he can grow in his faith even while he struggles. I have met those who have displayed the fruit of the Spirit even while they have regarded their condition with sorrow and contrition, unable to change. They are fellow pilgrims enroute to the heavenly city.

With care, I would like to suggest some basic processes, each of which takes time. One step may blend into another or may need to be repeated. But I believe that Christ is able to deliver individuals from both homosexual desires and actions.

1. *Come to Christ as you are.* It is quite natural (but wrong) to think that we have to become worthy in order for God to accept us. This harmful perception keeps people from coming to Christ, for it leads them to believe that He died for some sinners but not others.

Homosexuals and adulterers, along with all of us, must bask in the love of God; we all must be willing to open our lives to His grace, for He sees our deceitful hearts. God does not turn His back on those who believe in His Son.

> Just as I am, without one plea
> But that Thy blood was shed for me,
> And that Thou bidd'st me come to Thee,
> O Lamb of God, I come!
> I come!

Yes, come to God *as you are!*

2. *Be willing to let God change you.* For many the thought of changing their homosexual identity is far from their minds. Even if change came easily they would not accept it because it would disrupt their present lifestyle and relationships. For them, the best they can do is to continue to adjust to the homosexual lifestyle as best they can and enjoy it.

Others wish to change but have believed the cruel lie that change is impossible. This false notion, perpetuated by the radical homosexual movement and so favorably reported by the media, is one of the stumbling blocks for major change. As Edmund Bergler wrote in *Homosexuality: Disease or Way of Life?* "The homosexual's real enemy is . . . his ignorance of the possibility that he can be helped, plus his psychic masochism which leads him to shun treatment."[3]

When Christ asked the man, "Wilt thou be made whole?" it was not an idle question. If Christ were to heal him, he would have to accept responsibility for some radical adjustments in his lifestyle.

Thus to be free from homosexuality, one must ask: Am I willing to let God make the changes He desires?

3. New York: Collier, 1962, p. 277.

3. *Repent of any bitterness toward God or others.* Since, as we have learned, homosexuality grows best in the context of broken relationships, it is understandable that homosexuals often have deep-seated bitterness toward others, usually members of their own family. Parents especially are the targets of such resentment because of failures on their part in nurturing their children.

As previously explained, if a father molests his daughter, she grows up with those experiences stamped upon her soul. She probably will hate men and cringe when she is touched. She may then turn to her own gender as an expression of her sexual desires and need for love and affirmation.

A son may resent his mother, hate women, and turn to men for the attention and sexual expression he now craves. Whatever the scenario, most homosexuals can point to failures within their own families that contributed to their chosen lifestyle.

All of this produces bitterness toward others and toward God. This bitterness must be released in an act of repentance and faith: "Let all bitterness and wrath and anger and clamor and slander be put away from you, along with all malice. And be kind to one another, tender-hearted, forgiving each other, just as God in

Christ also has forgiven you" (Ephesians 4:31-32).

If you ask why we must be willing to repent of our anger, even though we struggle with desires we adopted because of the failures of others, think of it this way: If you were born into a family that was greatly in debt, the responsibility for payment would be passed on to you. Even though you would thus be influenced by the choices others made, you, as an heir, would be held responsible for payment.

I don't think that any one of us is truly repentant until we realize that we are held responsible for our inability to obey God. God holds us responsible even though we are by nature the children of wrath. Grace is never poured out until we come to the point of full contrition and humility.

David learned that lesson: "The sacrifices of God are a broken spirit; a broken and a contrite heart, O God, thou wilt not despise" (Psalm 51:17). There can be no excuses, no appeals to our genes or our environment. Repentance means that we take responsibility for every attitude and every choice. The homosexual must renounce his lifestyle, just as a drunkard or idolater must renounce his.

4. *Break the power of illicit sexual experiences.* I've already emphasized that sex binds two people together, body, soul, and spirit. The person who has had sexual experiences outside of marriage has been united to someone in an alien relationship. The power of those memories must be broken, so that the obligation to repeat the behavior is erased.

That can be done through renunciation; God is able to purify our memories, or at to least break "the power of cancelled sin," to quote the words of Charles Wesley. Past sin need not have dominion over us. That is best done in the presence of a counselor or supportive friend.

5. *Find a support group.* Seldom, if ever, can a person break the power of a homosexual lifestyle without help from others. One girl, struggling with lesbianism, wrote, "Good listening ears were few and far between. I desperately needed people who would listen to me—for hours on end at times. I didn't want pat answers. They were usually much too simplistic or naive to be helpful. I needed someone who would listen with God's patience and compassion."

Most people who come out of homosexuality say that they had a confidant whom they could trust, a friend who would be there to provide encouragement and hope even in the midst of failure. Sometimes these men and women need to know that they can call on that friend at any time, day or night.

We all need fellow believers with whom we have acceptance.

6. *Understand the fact of temptation.* Many people think that God should give them deliverance in an instant without any further struggle with temptations or desires. But Alcoholics Anonymous teaches its clients to say "I am an alcoholic" even after a person has not touched a drink in ten years. This organization understands a basic principle: *We will always be tempted to repeat behavior that at one time was our master.*

A pastor who for years struggled with a secret life of homosexuality was delivered from the bondage that had ensnared him. But later he said that there were times when there was no battle at all and times when the battle was "horrendous."

He writes:

> One thing I have now is the knowledge that Satan can no longer lie to me and tell me that it is just the way I am and that I have to live with it. There have been times when the thoughts have again sought to invade may mind, but now I have a

choice. I can refuse to allow them to remain. A few times I have allowed them to remain and when that happens, just a simple confession has destroyed them and again cleaned up my mind.... The stronghold of homosexuality has been broken but I continue to battle the thoughts.

Often believers give up too easily, believing the lie that they must continue to be homosexuals.

7. *Be prepared to believe what God says about you as a Christian.* Every homosexual has experienced some emotional deprivation that has driven him to seek sexual experiences with the same sex. He thinks that the word *homosexual* is a fundamental description of his personal identity, that it represents who he really is.

But the moment a person becomes a Christian, he receives a new identity in Christ. Through understanding the Word of God he must come to the conclusion that God has changed the core of his identity. Rather than being in Adam as all unbelievers are, the Christian who struggles with homosexuality is now "in Christ," with all rights and privileges that accompany such a change.

The key to overcoming any sin is for us to *disbelieve* what our emotions and thoughts tell us and to *believe* what God has said about us. Only such faith can take the victory of Christ and enforce it in our lives.

Scripture memory, though not a cure-all, is essential in changing these thought patterns.

8. *Be prepared for demonic warfare.* Because Satan is involved in immoral relationships, some Bible teachers have taught that deliverance from homosexuality simply involves exorcism, namely, the casting out of a demon of homosexuality.

However, I believe that homosexuality would exist even if God would confine the devil to another planet. Our fallen nature has within itself the capacity for all kinds of sins, of which homosexuality is but one.

Of course, demonic spirits do exploit all illicit sexual experiences, hoping to hold their victim bound by repeated sinful behavior. *That is why it is impossible to be delivered from homosexuality without encountering battles with demonic forces.* I encourage you to read *The Adversary,* by Mark Bubeck (Chicago: Moody, 1975).

My point is simply that Satan must be confronted *along with* the inner healing of the soul that comes through the power of the Holy Spirit and the people of God.

### THE WALK TO FREEDOM

Roger Montgomery, the male prostitute referred to earlier, discovered that there is is a way out of homosexuality. After his conversion he struggled with homosexuality for two years before he felt totally free, and eventually he married a woman with whom he had two children.

Unfortunately, his transformation took place after the AIDS virus had already infected his body. But before his death on November 6, 1989, he recorded a message, "The Walk To Freedom." Before I give a synopsis of the truths that helped him draw on God's resources to overcome his homosexuality, let me briefly recount his story.

Roger's struggle with homosexuality began when he was molested by an older homosexual neighbor. Though the experience was initially painful, soon he began to enjoy the encounters. His homosexual identity was strengthened by the male pornography his mother had in the home.

He thought that if he attended a Bible college, he would be able to overcome homosexuality. But he was dismissed because he continued this behavior. He began to hate and distrust God. He would actually curse God, and even told Him to get out of his life. He gave himself to Satan.

He was without a job and a home, so he turned to prostitution to support himself. This was coupled with cocaine and alcohol abuse. When his fear that he had AIDS was confirmed, he begged God to die.

In a moment of despair he heard the voice of Christ (not audibly), who offered him life instead of death. For the first time he realized that he could come to Christ just as he was, without having to change. There was no new leaf he had to turn over; he would simply come to God as he was. God did not merely offer him change, but a brand new life. At last he was converted.

Soon he had a job and a place to live. Though his struggle with homosexuality continued, the process of change began. He found a pastor and a support group that helped him through the healing process. "By then I realized," he says, "that God had taken me out of homosexuality but had not yet taken the homosexuality out of me."

The deliverance began to happen. Though he experienced much temptation, he eventually discovered that his aversion to women began to change and he became attracted to them. A few years later, he married.

"Homosexuals err when they think that homosexuality is the only sin they have in their lives," says Roger. "But homosexuality is the fruit of sin, not the root of it. There are other sins and attitudes that God has to deal with in order to be free. After I became a Christian, I would ask God when he would work on my sexual desires. But God kept working on my pride and coveteousness. But this was the root that had to be confronted before I was ready to yield to God regarding my homosexuality."

What made the transformation complete? Here are the facts of Scripture that pointed the way to his freedom. The central truth is that God has united us with Christ.

> Therefore we have been buried with Him through baptism into death, in order that as Christ was raised from the dead through the glory of the Father, so we too might walk in newness of life. For if we have become united with Him in the likeness of His death, certainly we shall be also in the likeness of His resurrection, knowing this, that our old self was crucified with Him, that our body of sin might be done away with, that we should no longer be slaves to sin. (Romans 6:4-6)

Our union with Christ is so complete that when Christ died, we died to sin. That means that God miraculously put us into Christ so that we participate in His death and resurrection. Christ died not only that we might be forgiven but that we might be free. The power of sin has been broken in our lives. Now sin need not have dominion over us.

When homosexuality reigns in a person's life, he cannot break its power. But Christ broke sin's power. Heterosexuality is not something to be worked for; it is to be received through Christ. Christ does not expect homosexuals to change themselves. He only expects them to believe the Word of God. If we think God cannot change us, we make Him a liar.

When we are saved, God does something new in our lives. We become a new person. But now we need to learn how to walk in a power that has already been given to us. Sin is no longer our master; it has been nullified.

Now that sin's power has been broken, we must choose our master. Will we obey God, or will we continue to pursue our homosexual lifestyle? The choice is ours.

In faith we should consider ourselves dead to sin; and then we must present our bodies to God (Romans 6:11, 13). This is not positive thinking, but resting on true historical facts that we can depend upon. This enables us to see ourselves from a new perspective. As we consider the old self to be dead, the new man within will grow and enable us to walk in the power of the Holy Spirit.

How shall we handle temptation? We can *find* our *heterosexual selves* almost immediately, but there will be *temptations*. We can become sensitive to the conviction of the Holy Spirit. We will know that we should put that magazine down or turn the television set off. We must obey those promptings.

Once again we must choose to believe what God has said about us. We must also trust the Holy Spirit who indwells us to bring the fruit of righteousness into our lives. This is not the product of self-will. If a farmer wants to see a tree bear fruit, branches must be pruned. God does this in our lives as an act of His love for us. It hurts, but the benefits are worth it. The Holy Spirit then produces the purity we seek. Then we can begin to walk in heterosexual wholeness.

We cannot overcome these things by willpower. When we fall into sin, there is no use trying to beat ourselves, but rather we should agree with God about our sins (1 John 1:9). That means that we can come to God and pour out all of our sins, without excuses or fear of rejection. There is *nothing* that we cannot reveal or talk to Him about. As many times as we fall, we must come to Him to receive forgiveness. If we fall ten times a day, we must come to Him to confess our sin ten times. Failure should never discourage us.

The legal basis on which God can forgive us is the death of Christ. Continual cleansing comes only with continual confession. There is no sin that is too great for God; He can cleanse us from all sins.

How can I get rid of immoral thoughts? Christian activities will not bring cleansing of the mind. The transformation is done by God as we present ourselves to Him. There is a metamorphosis, a change that is supernatural. We must continually see the Lord in the Word of God. We cannot behold Him if we neglect the Scriptures. This looking upon Christ means that the change will take place.

Roger says, "Christ is the only true heterosexual. If the truth were known, all men are sexual deviates. It is just a matter of degree. Christ is the only perfect man."

Christ left the church on earth so that all sinners would have a place of healing. Roger says that homosexuals should let believers help them to overcome homosexuality. They need accountability, someone in whom they can confide.

The God of Roger Montgomery is the God who is well qualified to deliver His people from their sins.

And He is the God of all who believe.

**Organizations That Help
Promote Sexual Healing**

Homosexual Anonomous
Fellowship Services (H.A.F.S.)
P.O. Box 7881
Reading, PA 19603
   (nationwide referral service for H.A. support groups)

Exodus International
P.O. Box 2121
San Rafael, CA 94912
   (referrals for Exodus agencies *only*)

Overcomers: A Christian Ministry
5445 N. Clark Street
Chicago, IL 60640
   (nationwide ministry; referrals for individuals, parents, spouses)

Spatula Ministry
P.O. Box 444
La Habra, CA 90631
   (ministry referrals for parents and family members)

Moody Press, a ministry of the Moody Bible Institute, is designed for education, evangelization, and edification. If we may assist you in knowing more about Christ and the Christian life, please write us without obligation: Moody Press, c/o MLM, Chicago, Illinois 60610.